ACHILLION

The Palace of Elisabeth

EDITIONS TOUBI'S ΕΚΔΟΣΕΙΣ

ATHENS 2002

Text: ELENI PALASKA - PAPASTATHI
ARTISTIC EDITOR: EVI DAMIRI
PHOTOGRAPHS: M. TOUBIS S.A. ARCHIVES

NISIZA KARELA - KOROPI 194 00, P.O. BOX: 209
Tel. 010-6029974, 010-6645548, Fax: 010-6646856
http://www.toubis.gr

ISBN: 960-540-446-X

Portrait of Elisabeth by Franz Xavier Winterhalter.

ΑΧΙΛΛΕΥΣ

CONTENTS

The western coastline of continental Greece is framed by the island complex of the Eptanisia (Seven Islands), also known as the islands of the Ionian Sea. To these islands belongs Corfu, the second largest after Kefalonia and the most northerly island of the complex.

Nature generously blessed this island with colours, with blue and green dominating, tightly bound. No artist could have rendered this combination of colours so perfectly.

The characteristics of Corfu are: the rich vegetation, the chiselled hills, the well-formed hug of the coast, the serene beaches, the crystal-clear waters, the beautiful villages, the rich olive groves, and a town which emanates an air of nobility.

The human spirit and hard toil have scattered monuments all over this island, reminders of its long history. Monuments that are witnesses to the flourishing of culture in this place remain from the classical era, the early Christian and Byzantine

period, the period of Venetian rule, right through to British and French occupation.

Mythology, history, legends and tradition merge in the clear atmosphere of Corfu, creating a pleasant dream-like confusion. This is where the magic of the island lies. This is Corfu's 'something else'!

At the cross-roads of civilisations, like a bridge between east and west, with a culture influenced by neighbouring Italy, yet with traditions and a soul purely Greek, Corfu has its own magical physiognomy. The island of the Phaiacians and of Nausicaa, where, as Homer tells us, Odysseus stopped to rest - a respite in the 'Odyssey' during his return to Ithaki - has much to offer the traveller. One traveler to Corfu was Elisabeth, in 1861, and the attraction she felt for the island was such that it led her to creating the 'Achillion.'

A visit to the palace of the Empress of Austria, which she herself dedicated to Achilles, a hero whom she admired, is a must.

Pontikonisi with the church of the Virgin of Vlachernon.

CHRONOLOGY OF THE

June 1861 Elisabeth visits Corfu for the first time. She passes through Gastouri and the estate of Petros Vrailas Armenis and is taken by the beauty of the place.

1888 The Empress is a guest of the widow of the Corfiot poet and diplomat Petros Vrailas Armenis at their villa at Gastouri.
She decides to buy the land.

1889 Elisabeth purchases the Vrailos land and neighbouring plots. The Italian architects Raphael Carito and Antonio Landi are commissioned to design a luxury royal villa.

1891 The Achillion is completed.

1889-1891 Decoration, purchase of works of art, commissioning of paintings and sculptors, painting of murals.

1898 Elisabeth is assassinated and the palace abandoned.

1908 Kaiser Wilhelm II buys the Achillieion and renovates it, renews the furnishings, builds the ‘House of the Knights’ in the gardens on the designs of Ernst Ziller and orders that the garden be looked after and have lighting added to it.

HISTORY OF THE ACHILLION

Local archaeological excavations begin.	**1911**
Outbreak of First World War. Wilhelm abandons Corfu and his beloved Achillion, never to return.	**1914**
French and Serbian troops take over Corfu and the Achillion becomes a military headquarters and hospital. Much damage is done.	**1915**
The building and its treasures come into the possession of the Greek state.	**1919**
It is leased by the company Kazina Ellados S.A. and renovated. A casino is opened on its two upper floors, whilst the ground floor is used as a museum.	**1962**
Taken over by the Greek Tourism Organisation.	**1983**
Full-scale renovation. Its rooms are used for the official dinner given for the heads of the European Union state during the summit that took place on Corfu during the Greek Presidency.	**1994**
Today the Achillion is run by the company Ellinika Touristika Akinita S.A., the major shareholder of which is the Greek Tourism Organisation. The same company also owns the casino, which has been moved to another building. The second floor is now free, and used for functions, whilst the museum continues to operate on the ground floor.	**Today**

ACHILLION
THE PALACE OF ELISABETH

Above: the coat-of-arms of the Achillion. Opposite: view of the palace.

Elisabeth was a lover of Greek mythology and history, and with the help of her teachers, she studied the Greek language. She was especially enamoured of the Homeric epics and often asked her teachers to read or translate lines from the Iliad or the Odyssey. Among the heroes whom she especially admired was Achilles. He was her role model because: "he represents the Greek soul, the beauty of the land and the people of this place." And moreover, because he "had contempt, as he passed like a cloud, for all the kings and all the customs and laws." This she wrote herself, explaining her admiration.

In honour of her famous hero, the Empress named her villa the Achillion. This is where she sought refuge after the death of her son Rudolf, and she stayed here from time to time until her own assassination in 1898.

Starting from Corfu, in a south-westerly direction, we pass the pretty village of Gastouri, 11.5 km. from the town. Two km. to the east of the village, on a little hill covered in vegetation, stands the palace of the "sad Empress," as her biographers often call her.

This is an impressive, neo-classical building, inside of which there is a combination of architectural styles, with Renaissance and Pompeian features. The Empress herself was involved in the decoration, and she chose as a coat-of-arms the dolphin with the crown that we see in the palace.

The word Achillion is written over the heavy iron garden gate. A notice in the wall tells us about the construction of the building under the supervision of Baron Bukovic. From the moment that the visitor walks through the gate, it is as though he or she has walked into the complex world of Greek mythology.

The owner made sure that most of the works of art, the interior decoration and sculptures that decorate the garden refer to the Greek myths. A dry stone wall protects the luscious-green garden. To the left of the gate is the ticket booth, the old porters' lodge, and the House of the Knights, a little building constructed when the Achillieon belonged to Kaiser Wilhelm II. As soon as we pass through the gate, we encounter three statues in a row that will surely catch our attention with their liveliness.

1

The first is the **Satyr Cymbalist**, or **Musician**, a bronze statue full of movement. The marble sculpture is of the **Future of Sailor**, representing a boy in half a boat examining a map and planning his journeys for the future. And, finally, the Capitoline Hermes, based on a sculpture by Lysippus. In Elisabeth's day, the Hermes was located in the position where the Dying Achilles now is. Wilhelm II ordered this changeover.

In the forecourt, a short distance from the palace, there is a two-storey building where the Empress's carriages and horses were kept. It later housed the elementary school of the village of Gastouri, and, finally, it was renovated in 1962 and became a guest house belonging to Baron Richthofen.

The building has a grand facade, as befits such a palace, with sculptures, ancient Greek columns, large verandas. Above the main entrance there is a

2

large balcony (1st floor) with two marble sculptures of the **Capitoline Centaurs** in its external corners. Two smaller balconies to the right and to the left have a richly-decorated roof and are framed with ancient Greek columns. The verandas on the second floor have four bronze sculptures in their corners of **nymphs** with their arms raised holding up the lights. On the veranda of the left side of the building, there is a **statue of Hermes** with winged shoes.

4

1. *The Future Sailor.*
2. *Hermes Resting.*
3. *The veranda with the centaurs and the nymphs dressed in flowers.*
4. *Hermes with the Winged Feet.*
5. *The Satyr Cymbalist.*

3

5

TOUR OF THE ACHILLION AND ITS TREASUES

A. THE MUSEUM

1

2

1, 2. Relief decoration representing Zeus throwing lightening at the Titans and Achilles (or Helios) on his chariot. Opposite: Wall-painting by Galoppi with representations of the Four Seasons and the Hours.

Entrance

Entrance to the museum - which takes up the whole of the ground floor - is through a splendid iron door with a bronze **relief** representing Zeus throwing lightening at the Titans, and of Achilles (or the Titan Helios) on his four-horsed chariot.

Four Doric columns hold up the roof, which also functions as the balcony for the first floor.

During the Kaiser's time, the entrance was surrounded by crystal, but this was removed in the renovation of 1962.

Reception Hall

A splendid hall opens before us as we pass through the central entrance of the building. The most impressive feature here is the symbolic representation of the **Four Seasons** and the **Hours** with a giant fresco by the Italian painter Galoppi, which covers part of the roof and was painted in 1891. The artist's talented hand depicts spring, summer, autumn and winter the form of joyful girls and angels, whilst the hours, dancing hand-in-hand jump out from the clouds. The artist truly surprises us with his inventiveness in this wonderful composition with a dream-like atmosphere. A similar fresco can be found on the roof of the Villa Borges in Rome and in a painting in the Hermitage Museum in St Petersburg. The fresco is framed by decorative elements inspired by the archaeological finds at Pompeii, with the dominating motif of the Sphinx.

One of the walls in this hall is adorned with engravings and a copy of a portrait of

Galloppi 1891

1

2

1, 2. Statuettes by the sculptor Heinemann of the goddess Athena and Hebe.
3. General view of the reception hall.

3

Elisabeth at age 27 by L. Jacoby. The original, a work by the German painter Winterhalter is in the palace of Hofburg. The **fireplace** is in the opposite wall. Above its dark marble are two little sculptures, works by the German sculptor Heinemann: the goddess of wisdom **Athena** and **Hebe**, goddess of youth. An elegant **gold-inlaid clock** stands between them.

Table lamps, wall lamps, a white writing desk, and a mirror complement the decoration and furnishing of the first hall of the Achillion. At the edge, two columns buttress the roof, and the corners to the left and to the right are graced by two turquoise **vases** made in Florentine porcelain. These bear reliefs of mythological scenes, copied from ancient cups.

2

1. The reception hall with the fireplace and the gold-inlaid clock.
2. Decorative vase of Florentine porcelain.

1

Galloppi 1891

Palace Staircase

The staircase leading to the upper floors begins behind the columns. The wide marble stairs are framed on either side by brass banisters decorated with mythological themes.

The bronze statues of Zeus and Hera at the foot of the palace staircase, and many other marble and plaster sculptures that grace the top steps at each floor and the banisters refer for yet one more time to the ancient Greek myths. Among them are Caryatids, Nymphs, Bacchae, Naeads, Silens, Maenads, Satyrs, Zeus, Niobe, Artemis, Phoebus, Aphrodite, Hermes, ancient trophies, Pan and his followers. The composition on the staircase was painted in Naples by the Caponeti family.

The mirrors that have been placed among the sculptures, the painted motifs that cover the walls and the ceiling of the staircase, and the perfect lighting add emphasis to the grandeur of the place.

1

1. Plaster sculptures which decorate the top stair of each floor.

2, 3. The bronze sculptures of Zeus and Hera on the bottom steps.

2

3

The Triumph of Achilles

The wall at the top of the staircase on the second floor is covered by a splendid painted composition, with dimensions of 4 x 10 metres. This is 'The Triumph of Achilles,' or 'The Triumphant Achilles,' oil on canvas, painted by the famous Austrian Franz Matz in 1892. Here, the artist has managed to render with dramatic precision the scene showing the procession of the body of Hector and the triumph of Achilles. The hands of the artist have turned Homer's lines from the Iliad into a living picture. Homer narrates and Matz represents on canvas.

As Homer tells us, during the siege of Troy, Hector fought a duel with Patroklus, the beloved friend of Achilles. He killed Patroklus and won the battle. To avenge the death of his friend, Achilles then fought a duel with Hector, killing the Trojan and dragging his dead body around the walls of Troy, in a burst of outrage, but also as a show of strength.

The central figure in the work, Achilles, is represented upright, standing triumphantly in his chariot. With a proud and haughty manner, the triumphant victor holds the trophy of the helmet, whilst in his other hand he holds his shield and spear. The helmet had originally been his, but he had given it to Patroklus to frighten the Trojans and Hector, having killed Patroklus, kept it as booty, something especially derogatory for Achilles. The dark-coloured steeds gallop furiously and their manes flutter behind them. Behind the hero is the driver, whose face is twisted from his efforts to calm the horses. The movement of the animals has been masterfully rendered and is one of the features - along with the perfect use of light and shade and the expressions of the faces - that have contributed to the opinion that 'The Triumph of Achilles' is the best work in the whole palace. The hero's chariot is followed by a second with white horses and his soldiers, the brave Myrmidons, who cheer him on for his victory and share in his triumph. The lifeless body of Hector is being dragged along by the hero's chariot. In the background, behind a curtain of dust swept up by the driving procession, the walls of Troy can just be seen and, inside, the Trojans who watch the horrific scene, unable to do anything.

Art critics have noted one flaw in this otherwise marvellous painting: the wheel of Achilles' chariot does not appear to be turning as it should in order to show movement. Others suggest that the artist used paintings of Roman chariot races as his models, in which the wheels appear motionless.

The Chapel

Sculpture of the Virgin Mary with the Holy Infant, a copy of the Virgin of Marseilles, the Notre Dame de la Garde, a work of the sculptor Polari.

With the opening of the door on the right-hand side of the reception hall, the visitor is immersed in an atmosphere of piety, entering an entirely different environment. This area was adapted, on Elisabeth's instructions, into a Catholic chapel. The Empress was a pious Christian and wished to have in her villa a special area in which she could communicate with God and release herself from the pain and misfortunes of her life.

The most important work in the chapel is the wall-painting in the dome, with the theme of the ***Trial of Christ***. Christ, surrounded by guards, accounts to Pontius Pilate. This exceptional work is unsigned, but is thought to have been painted by the Hungarian artist Michael Munkacsy, who had painted the same theme elsewhere in this period. The three-dimensional effect and the gold background behind the figures that lights up the scene make this work one of the most beautiful in the whole Achillion. Angels and various other decorative motifs are painted around the dome. Two plain columns and two elegant Corinthian columns support the dome. There are two sculptures in between the columns: **Christ (Sacred Heart)** and the **Virgin Mary (the Immaculate Conception)** placed in niches. In the centre of the cavity, beneath the Trial of Christ, is the ***Stella del Mare***. This is a painting by Franz von Matz, who painted the palace at Vienna. This work was commissioned by the Empress and is dedicated to the Virgin, who saved Elisabeth's yacht from a great storm at sea. It represents the Virgin with Christ in her embrace rising from the sea. The twelve stars in her halo symbolise the twelve tribes of Israel.

Beneath the painting is the icon stand, the altar and the organ. To the left, we see a sculpture of the **Virgin and Child** on a pillar. This is a copy of the Virgin of Marseilles, patron goddess of sailors, the *Notre Dame de la Garde*, a work by the Italian painter Polari.

The chapel is graced with relief sculptures on the walls: **Saint Genaro** (alabaster), **the Virgin and Christ** (marble with a gold halo), the **Birth of Christ and the Virgin and Christ** (both in porcelain, by the Florentine

F. MATSCH

«Ο Θριαμβεύων Αχιλλεύς», έργο του Αυστριακού ζωγράφου Φραντς Ματς.

The Triumph of Achilles.

1

Delarobia brothers), the **Meeting of the Virgin with the Mother of St John the Baptist**.

Paintings of Catholic popes and Orthodox priests round off the wall decoration inside the chapel.

Finally, priestly vestments given to the pious Empress by Pope Pius IX are kept in an old wardrobe.

1. The Meeting of the Virgin with the Mother of St John the Baptist.
2, 4. Wall-paintings from the chapel.
3. Delarobia brothers' relief of the Virgin and Christ.

2

3

4

ST MARIA

Room with Mementoes of Elisabeth

1

In this room, which is next to the chapel, we will find mementoes of Elisabeth, primarily small objects that belonged to her and a few items of furniture, from which we can draw information about her life.

Most of the furniture is white - desks, armchairs, cabinets and a strange, round, little white table which is supported by sculptures of Caryatids.

The photographs are of interest: in one, both she and her husband the Emperor are shown on horseback, another shows her alone at the age of 59, two years before her assassination. There are also photographs of her statue, which stands in the forest of the Achillion, the cenotaph of her son Rudolf, an album with photographs of the Achillion, a rare volume with the biography of Franz Josef, poems written in Gothic script for the first anniversary of their engagement and, directly next to it, a copy of a

2

painting by Franz von Matz showing her husband receiving Wilhelm II and other German leaders during the celebrations for the sixtieth anniversary of his reign in Vienna.

Interesting copies of two lithographs of Elisabeth at age 17 and of Franz Josef at age 24 - the ages they were at their wedding - hang on the wall. A portrait of Elisabeth, painted by an unknown artist in pen and ink, graces one of the walls of the room. In this painting the Empress is 29-years-old. To the left and to the right of it are framed documents, photocopies and photographs about her assassination. There are two candlesticks and two clocks, with a tray in between them with a drawing of the Miramar palace, which belonged to Franz Josef's brother.

Of the small objects in this room, we can mention the commemorative medals, the murano jugs, two miniature busts of herself and the Emperor, the cast of a statue of the Empress, the wonderful Italian porcelain jug made by the Capodimonte workshop, and two poems composed by the Empress herself.

Finally, in one corner, there is a bust of Franz Josef set up on a base.

1. Poem written on the occasion of the first anniversary of Elisabeth and Franz Joseph.
2. Dresser with objects belonging to Elisabeth.
3. Small table with a Caryatid leg.
4. Vase made from Italian porcelain in the Capodimonte workshop.

3

4

Room with Mementoes of Wilhelm II

1

1. The actual flag from the yacht.
2. Miniature representation of the Imperial yacht, the Hohenzollern.
3. Wilhelm's desk and the portrait by Stover of the Emperor in German naval uniform.

From the exhibits in this room, we can draw information about the life of the villa's next owner, Kaiser Wilhelm II of Germany and King of Prussia, and also about life at the Achillion under his ownership. Wilhelm is shown in the uniform of a Captain of the German navy in a photograph by Stover.

The three watercolours of ships that frame the portrait are also by the same painter.

The seat in front of Wilhelm's small white desk is quite curious - it is in fact a saddle set up on a base. It is said that the Emperor would use such 'seats' on which to sit upon - he had one in each of his residences - because he felt more comfortable, but also more like a leader. Perhaps, in addition, whenever he sat on this seat he felt as though he was enjoying his favourite sport, horseriding. The porcelain stove nearby is a rare piece. The toilet with the wash-basin and the carved Venetian mirror from Elisabeth's day, complete the furnishings in this room.

Of especial interest are the rare photographs hung on the walls, as they provide us with valuable information on the history of the period. In one of these, the blue-blooded members of various European Royal families pose in front of the camera. In another photograph, we learn how the various sections of the statue of the Victorious Achilles were brought to the palace and assembled in the garden of the Achillion.

A third photograph shows the archaeological excavations on the island.

Commemorative fine porcelain plates, honorary medals, military medallions, dinner sets, a Prussian escutcheon, bronze busts of the grandfather and father of Wilhelm and other mementoes of the Hohenzollern family are displayed in an exhibition case.

There is a fine painting by the Corfiot painter Georgios Samartzis to the right of the exhibition case. This is the portrait of Ferdinando Botemo, the general director of the Achillion.

On a base, projecting, we see a miniature of the imperial yacht the Hohenzollern, of which the Emperor was especially proud. On the wall above the perfect hull of the Hohenzollern is framed the actual flag of the yacht, with the cross, the slogan Gott Mit Uns, the escutcheon, the Imperial crowns and the year 1871, when Germany was united with Prussia.

2

On the wall also are telegraphs sent by Wilhelm from Doorn in Holland, where he was living in self-exile. There are also photographs of the Kaiser himself at the Achillion, as he had designed it. Next to these is a small cast of the *Victorious Achilles*.

Our tour of this wing of the Achillion ends here.

1

We now proceed in the direction of the other wing of the palace. The first room on this side - a smoking room in the imperial years - today functions as an office. A section of the fresco by an unknown artist on the ceiling is still preserved, depicting **Eros and Pysche**, with ornate decoration around the edges.

1. *Fresco of Eros and Psyche.*
2. *General view of the dining room.*

2

3

4

Elisabeth's Dining Room

3. Venetian mirror.
4. Plaster designs of Cupids.

We now find ourselves in the Empress's dining room, where items belonging to the palace's two former owners are exhibited. In Elisabeth's day this room was especially grand, as we can see from the old photographs. The ceiling was richly decorated with plaster reliefs of animals. All that remains of this splendid decoration today is the ornate border, as well as the decoration of the walls, with **plaster designs of Baroque-style Cupids**.

The most impressive feature in this room today is the completely-carved Italian marble **fireplace** with mythological subjects.

There is an old clock set up on the marble above the fireplace, whilst on the wall above this we can admire Elisabeth's portrait. The Empress is beautiful in this, in full bloom at the age of 25.

This painting is a copy - the original is in Munich - and it was painted by the German artist Franz Srotsberg in 1862.

On another wall of this room there is a portrait of Elisabeth's husband Franz Josef at a young age, also a copy. Beneath the painting is his sword. A carved **Venetian mirror** which belonged to Elisabeth, a white desk and chair with a curved back, as well as other small tables and chairs from the Kaiser's day complete the furnishing and decoration of this room, yet without being able to convey the grandeur which once characterised it.

An engraving in the hallway outside this room depicts the Old Fortress of Corfu in the days of Venetian rule.

Sculpture Room

A smaller area has been created next to the dining room where four marble reliefs and a statue, artists unknown, are exhibited, all inspired by Greek mythology. Four of these had been commissioned and purchased by Elisabeth, whilst the other had been donated to the Kaiser in 1913. The first relief, starting from the right, represents the happy band of **Dionysus and his escort**. The second refers to the well-known myth of the quarrel between the three goddess, Athena, Hera and Aphrodite, over the Apple of Discord. Aphrodite is provocatively displaying the apple that Paris had given her, and thus proclaiming her the most beautiful. In the third relief, **a winged Cupid embraces Helen of Troy** in an attempt to convince her to follow Paris.

In the fourth relief, a gift to the Kaiser, **Orpheus and Eurydice** emerge from Hades accompanied by Hermes psychopompos, the conductor of souls to the Underworld. This relief is a copy of a Roman original in the Louvre. The fifth is a sculpture of the poet **Sappho** - also known as the Tenth Muse - with her hair caught in some rocks. It represented the moment of her suicide, which took place, according to the myth, at the cape of Lefkata on the island of Lefkada.

The marble reliefs of the Sculpture Room:

1. *Dionysus and his escort.*
2. *The poet Sappho.*
3. *Orpheus, Eurydice and Hermes.*
4. *Athena, Hera and Aphrodite with the Apple of Discord.*

1

2

3

4

Room with Elisabeth's Desk and Bookcase

This room contains valuable items of furniture that belonged to the Empress, and which bear the mark of her own personal taste, as well as small items and mementoes of the Kaiser. The main exhibits in this room are Elisabeth's desk and bookcase, both of which are finely carved. Griffin heads have been carved onto the legs of the splendid desk, the symbols of imperial power.

The same design appears on the legs of her armchair. There are signs in Morse code on the desk. The bookcase is fully carved, with inlaid heads of the goddesses Demeter, Persephone, Athena and Hera.

A collection of poems written in gothic script by Heinrich Heine, the Empress's beloved poet, is kept on the shelves. There are also two biographies of Wilhelm, a book on the Achillion that was written by Elisabeth's teacher Constantine Christomanos, and photographs of the members of the Hohenzollern family are kept

1. General view of the room.
2. Statuette of Hermes on the bookcase.
3. Bronze bust.
4. Wood-carved commode with Wilhelm's terracotta ashtray.

1

on the shelves. Two little statues decorate the upper part of the bookcase. On the other side of the room there is a commode of excellent craftsmanship and two bedside tables that belonged to Elisabeth. They are wood-carved with delicate marquetry and meander patterns, and representations of cupids, dolphins, and sphinxes. An ashtray that belonged to Wilhelm has been placed on top of the commode. It is made of terracotta and is from the Capodimonte workshop. The sculptures on exhibit in this room are quite splendid. They are all copies of originals on exhibit in museums in Naples and the Vatican. Most are bronze. We start from Homer, moving to Aeschines, the wrestler cleaning himself with a scraper - copy of a work by Lysippus - Epicurus, Hesiod, Sappho (or Hera), Hermes and an unidentifiable sculpture with a wooden face.

2

There is also a case in which we can admire copies of the crown jewels, the originals of which are kept in the palace in Vienna.

On the wall above the bookcase hangs a painting of Wilhelm II on his yacht, a work of Bruno Pinkas.

To the right of the painting is a sword that once belonged to the Emperor.

On the wall above Elisabeth's commode are hung two German banners from the war against the French that the Germans won in '1870-71'.

3

4

Furniture from Elisabeth's Bedroom

We now find ourselves in the last room of the museum, which contains primarily furniture and objects from Elisabeth's bedroom. The two great **wardrobes** are the most impressive items in here. One has a central door with a crystal mirror, with two doors to the right and left adorned with fine marquetry. On the upper part there is a carved wooden head of the Medusa with a chiselled decoration of dolphins and meanders. The other wardrobe also features ornate wood-carved imagery.

1

One of the rarer items in the palace is the cover of an old stove that the Empress brought back from a trip to Constantinople.

Also of interest are the many **mirrors** of different sizes and styles that we encounter in this room - an essential feature, in any case, among a lady's personal objects. A small, gold mirror from Venice hangs from the walls.

The large, golden, oval-shaped mirror, which belonged to Elisabeth's personal toiletries, is carved all over with vegetation patterns and has two griffins carved into its legs.

A slightly smaller mirror in the opposite corner is also wood-carved, with a walnut-colour varnish. It stands on two carved legs, with two dolphins at the bottom. The mirror over the wash-basin is rectangular with a carved wooden frame with meander patterns and the head of the Medusa in relief at the top. The mirror stands upon the light-brown marble of the splendid wash-basin, which also has Medusa heads and meander marquetry.

It is said that the Empress had a weakness for mirrors but that she was also superstitious of them. One typical story mentions that as she was leaving the Achillion a little before her assassination, she saw that her favourite gold mirror had cracked, and said to herself "I will never see the Achillion again," seeing the crack in the mirror as a bad sign.

1. Ceramic pot with arabesque designs.
2. Carved wardrobe with a crystal mirror.
3. Gold-inlaid wood-carved mirror.
4. General view of the room with the painting The Meeting of Odysseus with Nausicaa by the artist Thiers.

Elisabeth would relax and read on the Roman-style sofa with the feet carved in the form of dolphins. The large ceramic pot with finely-worked arabesque designs and Arab script on enamel and gold belonged to the Kaiser, a gift from an Arab King on one of the Emperor's journeys to the east.

The exceptionally elegant desk with fine marquetry and wonderful carvings is one of the most delightful pieces of furniture in this last room of the museum.

Finally, one of the most important exhibits in this room, and one of the most beautiful paintings in the palace collections, is the large oil painting, an original by the Bavarian painter Ludowig Thiers: ***The Meeting of Odysseus with Nausicaa***. The talented hand of this experienced artist - a professor at the School of Fine Arts in Athens in 1859 - has represented one of the scenes described by Homer in the 'Odyssey' with imagination and sensitivity. Odysseus, exhausted, had come onto the dry land and fallen asleep on a deserted beach on Scheria, which some believe to be today's Corfu. He was suddenly awoken by the voices and laughter of girls playing. This was Nausicaa, the daughter of King Alcinous, and her escort. At the sight of the naked stranger, the girls ran away. The princess, however, bravely approached him and offered him the red chiton from her shoulders to cover himself with. Odysseus, leaning before her, attempted to hide his naked body and at the same time make a sign of gratitude in response to Nausicaa's offer. The princess is rendered with a natural simplicity, and appears composed and noble, emotions that are evoked by her lowered gaze.

2

3

Here ends the tour of the Museum of the mementoes of Elisabeth and Wilhelm.

4

The peristyle of the Muses.

B. THE PALACE GARDENS

After the visit to the museum, a walk in the palace gardens is a must. The gardens are an integral part of the building and are, in the opinion of many, the most charming section of the palace.

Rich vegetation, ancient palm trees, flower-beds that are cared for with flowers of many colours and, in among them, sculptural compositions that refer us to Greek mythology and history, elegant columns, monuments, busts of philosophers, poets and

The entrance to the gardens of the Achillion.

politicians, verandas and viewing points with an unlimited view, the serenity of Nature in all its grandeur... All these harmoniously co-exist in the gardens of the palace, creating a dream-like environment.

As we leave the palace, we encounter the stairway of the Olympian Gods. The statues of four gods stand on large marble columns to the right and the left of a magnificent staircase: Apollo, God of music and light; Hermes, the herald and conductor of souls to the Underworld; Artemis, the goddess of hunting; and Aphrodite, the goddess of beauty and love.

The Peristyle of the Muses

From the stairway we are led to the Peristyle of the Muses. Elisabeth thought of this space as "her new Olympus."

The Peristyle of the Muses is a covered L-shaped stoa, or veranda, the cover of which is held up by Ionian columns. In front of each column, there is a statue standing on a low pedestal. The first, at the entrance to the peristyle, represents Apollo holding a lyre in his left hand.

There follow the **Three Graces**, the daughters of Zeus and Eurynome: Euphrosyne, Thalia and Aglaia. These were minor goddesses, patrons of the joy of life and pleasure. They were responsible for Aphrodite's adornment and ministrations, and organised the celebrations of the Olympian gods. The statue of Euphrosyne - here represented as a dancer with a light step, her hands held gracefully at the waist and with her dress raised - is a work of the Italian sculptor Canova.

After the Graces, in the corner of the Peristyle, there is a sculpture of a young woman with an open book - perhaps the Bible - held in her hands, representing Christian Philosophy.

We then encounter the ***Nine Muses*** one-by-one. These were the daughters of Zeus and Mnemosyne who, according to mythology, were the protectors of letters, the arts and science. In order, then, we have: Melpomene the Muse of tragedy, Terpsichore the Muse of dance and choral poetry, Euterpe (lyric poetry), Ourania (astronomy), Erato (love), Clio (history), Polymnia (religious poetry), Kalliope (epic poetry). Each Muse holds in her hands an object related to the science or art over which she is patron. Some of the sculptures of the Muses had been bought by Elisabeth from the

Below: Some of the Nine Muses.
Above (p. 45) The Three Graces.

1

2

Villa Borges, whilst the others are creations of the Italian sculptor Morani. The series of sculptures in the Peristyle closes with a small winged Cupid seated in front of the last column.

The Stoa

Along the wall of the Stoa formed within the Peristyle there are the **busts** of thirteen great men of antiquity, as well as the English playwright Shakespeare, whom the Empress especially admired. They are positioned on marble half-columns, which act as pedestals. Starting from the left, we read their names chiselled onto the statues in Greek letters, aside from that of Shakespeare: Demosthenes the Athenian, the greatest rhetorician of ancient Greece, the tragic poet Sophocles, Shakespeare, the rhetorician Lysias, the pupil of Epicurus Metrodoros, Plato, Homer, Carneades - a philosopher from Cyrene – the youngest of the tragic poets Euripides, Periandros the Corinthian - one of the seven wise men - the Stoic philosopher Zeno, the Cynic Antisthenes and, finally, Cicero's teacher Poseidon.

There is a delightful sculpture outside of the outer door of the second floor, which leads into the Peristyle, and which reminds us of the myth of **Leda and the swan**. According to this myth, Zeus could not resist the charms of the beautiful Leda, wife of Tyndareus, King of Sparta, and he wanted to conquer her. The father of the gods, notorious for his extra-marital affairs, transformed himself into a swan and flew into the arms of his beautiful beloved. From this erotic embrace was born Helen of Troy and the Dioscuri, Castor and Pollux. The marble sculpture represents Leda as half-naked - only her legs are covered by a pleated chiton - and her face is lit up with a sweet smile, as she tenderly holds the swan.

In closing this description of the Peristyle and the Stoa, we should mention the grandeur that characterised them in Elisabeth's day. In old photographs, we can see that the ceiling of the stoa bore painted decoration in brilliant colours, whilst the walls were covered in murals with mythological and historical subjects. This very spot today, along the longest length of the wall, has instead been taken up by large balcony doors. On an old postcard with a caption we see Homer telling his epic poems to a child sat next to him, and this scene was one of the old wall paintings from the Stoa. On the walls there were also depictions of Apollo, Daphne, Theseus, scenes from Aesop's fables, etc. The Stoa must have been incredible, especially in the evenings when it would have been lit by a row of lamps. This painted decoration on the ceiling and walls of the Stoa was removed with the first renovation conducted in the time of Wilhelm (1907), and also with the second renovation of 1962. The ceiling today bears a relief decoration that has been added later.

One of the works of arts that no longer stands here is a marble sculpture of the Neread of light Peri. In old photographs of the Peristyle, we can see that this sculpture was positioned at the edge of the Stoa, there where the row of columns ended, set up on an oval pedestal. The naked Neread lay nonchalantly upon the wings of a swan, tenderly holding a baby in her arms.

Busts from the Stoa of the Wise Men: Homer, Lysias, Sophocles, Demosthenes, Zeno, and Euripides. Left: Sculpture of Leda and the Swan.

The Garden of the Muses

The area within the L-shape that is formed by the columns of the Peristyle is known as the Garden of the Muses. This is a spacious, paved raised forecourt from which there is a wonderful view. One side of it has a semi-circular balcony with a marble bench and table. In Elisabeth's day, as we can see from old photographs, the balcony was covered with a canopy that bore ancient-style decorative elements and was held up by iron poles. Harps had been placed on top of the poles, and they would reverberate with heavenly melodies whenever the wind blew. Elisabeth would often come here to enjoy the wide, open view and the divine music; as she looked over at

1

2

3

the cenotaph of her son, she would mourn over his unjust death.

There is a small lake in the centre of the Garden of the Muses, within which there is a strange bronze sculpture of a dolphin wrapped around the body of the drowning **citharode Arion** in an attempt to save him. Around the lake, on a marble pedestal, there is another bronze statue of a **Satyr with the young Dionysus in his arms**, a work of the German sculptor Ernst Herter. The Satyr is preparing to sounds the cymbals that he holds in his hands, reminding us of the cymbalist musician whom we met in the forecourt in front of the palace. There is a small marble sculpture on the same pedestal.

Near the last column of the Peristyle, the boundary of the Garden of the Muses is defined by two of the most important statues of the Achillion, which have been stood opposite each other. These are the **Pouncing Wrestlers**, works by an unknown artist, copies of those in the Museum of Naples, which are distinguished for their movement and liveliness. They represent two wrestlers during a bout, ready to pounce upon each other. With the pronouncement of the left leg, the delicate extension of the right hand and the bend of the body forwards, the sculptor was able to breath life into the soulless bronze.

1. The Veranda of Tears.
2. Arion the Citharode and the sculpture of the Satyr with the young Dionysus.
3. The Pouncing Wrestlers.

The Garden of the Dying Achilles

The stairs that commence between the pedestals of the wrestlers lead us to a lower garden, right in the centre of which the Dying Achilles is today to be found.

This is a sculptural masterpiece, undoubtedly the most superior in the Achillion not just from an artistic perspective, but also in terms of its symbolism in relation to the palace. It has been praised in the international press, and copies of it are to be found in the Academy of Arts and National Gallery at Berlin. It is a work of the German sculptor Ernst Herter, professor of sculpture at the Academy of Arts at Berlin. The artist often drew the subject matter for his compositions from Greek mythology and history. Other well-known sculptures of his with an ancient Greek theme are the Antigone and Alexander the Great.

According to the myth, Thetis, the mother of Achilles, would wash her son's hair in the waters of the sacred spring of the Helmus so as to make him invulnerable. The hero did indeed become immortal, but vulnerable only in the heel of his right foot, as this is where his mother would hold him as she dipped him into the water. From the Iliad, we learn that before Paris – the son of Priam, King of the Trojans - fought Achilles in the duel, Apollo, who was on the side of the Trojans, revealed to Paris the secret of Achilles' heel. So, Paris aimed for Achilles' heel, hit his target, and killed him.

At an exhibition in Vienna in 1881, the attention of the art-loving Elisabeth was caught by a small plaster sculpture by Herter, with the subject of Achilles wounded by Paris' deadly arrow. Moved by this composition, she commissioned the artist to create a marble, life-size sculpture with the same theme. The result, which was quite justly to the Empress's satisfaction, was the Dying Achilles.

The sculpture was purchased in 1884 and brought to the palace at Vienna, and then to the hunting lodge of Lainster. When the palace at Corfu was completed in 1891, it seemed self-evident that the natural place for this sculpture was in the gardens here, and it might even have given Elisabeth the original spark of inspiration for naming the palace the Achillion, in addition to the admiration in which she held the hero.

Elisabeth ordered that it be placed on the last rooftop of the Achillion, and she would spend many hours next to it reading lines from the Iliad. The sculpture was moved to its present location in the days of Wilhelm. The Empress also had a similar sculpture at the Villa Miramar.

The warrior, wounded by Paris' arrow, is half-lying on the long and narrow pedestal. Very little of his body is covered by his pleated chiton, and the spasms of his muscles from the pain and anxiety can quite clearly be seen. He supports his body, stretched backwards, with his broad chest thrust out, on his left hand. With his right

hand, he holds the arrow that has been stuck into his 'Achilles' heel' and is attempting to remove it, in a last, desperate attempt. His wounded leg is stretched out and the muscles are perfectly inscribed upon it.

The most amazing thing about this sculpture is the expression on the face of the hero as he is about to die. A mixture of pain, desperation, anger, outrage, pride and bravery. We must not forget that he is a demi-god, a hero, but also human. His beautiful head, ringed with his rich hair and the honorary crown of the Myrmidons, turns towards his left shoulder. His lips, half-open, appear to be expressing a cry of agony and anger. In his sad eyes is imprinted the passion for the life which he feels is leaving him. He struggles to keep the dignity that befits a hero. He does not beg, he is not humbled, because "he is strong, proud and as stubborn as a Greek mountain." This moment is the moment of the last breath of one of the leading heroes of the Iliad, imprinted upon the cold marble with great vibrancy and romanticism by the magical hands of a talented artist. The proportions of the body are totally harmonised, the lines of the muscles on the haunches, the legs, the arms and the shoulders are perfect, the undulations of the back and waist, the nerve which is inscribed on his neck, are all absolutely realistic.

The Dying Achilles.

1

2

The Gardens of the Victorious Achilles

We descend the stairs from the Garden of the Dying Achilles, to find ourselves in the last garden of the palace, where the giant statue of the Victorious Achilles stands tall.

Next to the stairs, we meet two Italian-style sculptures. One represents the **Hesperides** and the other Summer in the form of the goddess of agriculture **Demeter**. This sculpture was stolen in 1994, but was recovered and placed once more in its position. The two marble baths nearby belong to the palace.

At another point in the last garden of the Achillion, the naked beauty of **Phryne**, a work by the German sculptor F. Heinemann, attracts our attention. This is a marble statue of the beautiful courtesan from Thespe who lived during the 4th century BC and who was known by the name Mnesarete. Her beauty was so great and the proportions of her body so perfect that leading sculptors and painters of the era such as Praxiteles and Apelles used her as a model for their statues of Aphrodite. When the courtesan, who was well acquainted with artistic and political circles, was accused of impiety, she was defended by the celebrated rhetorician Hyperides. Indeed, it is said that at the end of his speech he pulled her chiton from her revealing her wonderful body to the dumbfounded jurists - her beautiful features thus making the case for her acquittal! The sculpture that we have before us most probably represents this particular scene. Phryne is depicted naked, holding her chiton in one hand, whilst the other moves complacently towards her hair. She has a light step and the provocative stance of her perfectly-formed body reveals an exhibitionist tendency.

At one edge of the garden, near to the ancient courtesan and behind a small, closed door that led to the forest, there is another important sculpture in the garden of Achilles. This is a marble statue of **Lord Byron**, known for his philhellenic tendencies and his

3

4

stand in the Greek War of Independence against the Turks. This is a work of an unknown artist that Elisabeth, who admired the philhellene poet, purchased. She was moved by his romantic poems, and she had much in common ideologically with the English Lord.

The poet is seated in a position of recollection or deep contemplation, with his arm leaning against the back of the seat and his hand raised to his head. The marks of intellect and noble descent are imprinted on his face. His clothes are rendered in great detail. This piece is considered to be quite a rare one in the art collection of the Achillion from a thematic as well artistic perspective, given that it is one of the few pieces that is not inspired by Greek antiquity.

Another Achilles awaits us in the clearing of the final garden, among the tall, ancient palm trees. This is the statue of the **Victorious Achilles**, a work that is remarkable more for its style than its artistic value. It is 5.50 metres tall - 11.5 metres if we count its podium and spear - and weighs 4.5 tons, whilst the spear is 7.5 metres long. It is a work of the German sculptor Getz, who initially created, on order of the Kaiser, a cast that is on exhibit in the room with the mementoes in the palace. The Emperor approved it and the artist proceeded with the commission. Of great interest is the way in which this giant statue was transported, as we can see in the old photographs of the museum. It was constructed in several sections that were brought over to Corfu in 1909. The pieces were assembled here on the site previously occupied by the Dying Achilles.

1. *The statue of Phryne.*
2. *The marble statue of Lord Byron.*
3. *Demeter, the goddess of agriculture.*
4. *The Hesperis, a daughter of the night.*

The Emperor chose this prominent position on the edge of the final garden of the palace, as the most ideal for such a striking sculpture, and ordered that the Dying Achilles be moved to its present position. He considered the Victorious Achilles as his own and wanted to display it, as it represented for him the glory and strength of the warrior and the greatness of victory - ideals which he admired and which he had set as goals for his people. The powerful monarch considered the kingdom of the Myrmidons as a symbol of military virtue, as the ancient Greeks meant it. His hero was not a warmonger, but a worthy warrior and an exemplary leader. These were the characteristics that inspired Wilhelm.

The Emperor expressed his admiration for his hero with the Greek inscription carved in gold letters on the marble podium of the statue: "*Here is Achilles son of Peleus, whom the Emperor of the Germans Wilhelm set up, to be remembered for posterity.*" This inscription was erased by the French during the First World War as the statue was considered militaristic and the inscription provocative. All that remained was the name of the hero in capital Greek letters on the podium.

The Emperor would spend many hours in the garden of the Victorious Achilles, working near his beloved sculpture or enjoying the boundless view over the gulf.

The bronze warrior stands proudly on his base and gazes haughtily ahead. His lofty stance indicates that he is not concerned about the outcome of the war, he is certain that he will be the victor. His head is slightly raised and his charming face is full of self-confidence. He chest, stretched out, and his left leg, projected forward, indicate his readiness. Achilles is prepared for the battle

The statue of the Victorious Achilles.

and for victory. Fully armed, in his right arm he holds his spear and in his left the famed shield with which he had protected his body from the enemy weapons in many duels. In the centre of the shield there is a relief of the head of the Medusa, a symbol of power. Helmet, breastplate, sword and greaves complete the warrior's armour. The tip of his spear and the helmet had once been painted in gold so that they would shine from afar and be visible to those entering the port.

The Kaiser's love for and knowledge of ancient Greece were remarkable. In one old photograph, the Emperor can be seen at an archaeological site on Corfu, following the excavations.

The artistic value of the statue has been doubted, its giant proportions have inspired negative comment. Even so, we must allow that it is a remarkable work, a symbol of the palace and a mark left by Wilhelm of his time here.

Despite the fact that they represent the same person, the two statues of Achilles, the Dying Achilles and the Victorious Achilles, are quite unalike. They immortalise two different moments in the life of the same hero, and his reactions are diametrically opposed.

In the first statue, Elisabeth's beloved hero is a common mortal who is living his final moments with dignity. In the second statue, the Kaiser's hero lives his victory with excitement and pride. By comparing the two statues, we can see the difference in the attitudes of the two monarchs, both owners of the Achillion. The Dying Achilles is certainly a sculpture of exceptional skill, something that cannot be said for the Victorious Achilles.

With this description of the Victorious Achilles, our walk through the gardens of the Achillion comes to and end.

C. THE FOREST OF THE ACHILLION

A thick forest spreads out around and about the palace, past which the gulf that was used as a harbour by the Royal yachts expands. Entrance to the forest is prohibited today. A heavy iron gate and a splendid marble staircase led from the gardens to the forest, and from there to the harbour. A mole had at first been constructed here and later, in the Kaiser's day, a bridge - the Kaiser's Bridge - was added, which connected the mole with the gate. The mole terminated in two marble-sculpted dolphins, a symbol found often in Elisabeth's palace. The dolphins have been destroyed, and only a section of the mole and the stairs survive today.

The Statue of Elisabeth

On a raised area within the forest, near to the gate that led to the coast, there is a marble kiosk. This is known as the Temple of Heine or the Peristyle of Elisabeth. A set of steps leads to this impressive raised structure, which is made up of a peristyle with six Ionian columns holding up its elegant dome. A bronze sculpture of Nike with her wings spread adorns the dome. Within the kiosk there is today a simple sculpture of the sad Empress. It was set up here by the Kaiser in the position of the sculpture of one of Elisabeth's beloved poets, Heinrich Heine, a

1. The old entrance to the Achillion with the Temple of Heine.
2. Old photograph showing the entrance to the Achillion.
3. Old photograph of the statue of Elisabeth.

1

work of the Danish Sculptor Haselriis. Haine 'provoked' with his satirical poems Wilhelm and so the Emperor made sure when he bought the palace in Corfu, along with the other changes he made, to remove the statue of the poet. Today it can be found in a park in the French city of Toulon. As a substitute for this statue, Wilhelm placed a statue of his predecessor within this light and airy peristyle, showing in this way his admiration and respect for her.

Beneath the peristyle, there where the steps end, in a niche in the wall, there is another sculpture: the headless body of a woman wearing a rich, pleated chiton.

The sculpture of Elisabeth was a work of the renowned Austrian sculptor and professor of the Academy of Fine Arts at Vienna E. Helmer. Helmer had also made a similar scuplture of Elisabeth that is in Salzburg in Austria. We saw a mould of it in the museum. As we have seen, the Kaiser had a fondness for giant statues. And here, as with the statue of the Victorious Achilles, the dimensions are larger than life.

The Empress is represented standing upright, approachable and very human. With great skill and sensitivity, the artist has imprinted on the soulless marble the figure of a normal woman who has felt the pain of being deprived of a loved one. Elisabeth is shown as a simple bourgeois woman of her era, with her hair gathered, and her head uncovered and turning towards the left, as though she was waiting for someone coming in this direction. She may have been sorrowfully looking on at the cenotaph of Rudolf, which was located in this forest. Her hands are gently folded in front of her and her simple dress, which reaches down to the floor, delineates her erect poise. She does not wear any of the imperial symbols or crown jewels, only a cross, a gift from her dead son.

This image of Elisabeth from the peristyle in the forest is completely different from all those we have encountered inside the palace, either in paintings or as sculptures.

2

3

The Cenotaph of Rudolf

Near the Kiosk or Temple of Heine (today's Peristyle of Elisabeth) the Empress had one particular monument built that she visited every day: the Cenotaph of Rudolf. It no longer stands in the forest of the Achillion as it was removed by Franz Joseph to Vienna after Elisabeth's death and the sale of the villa to the Kaiser.

As we can tell from the old photographs that have been preserved and are on exhibit in the museum, this imposing yet at the same time simple monument is very emotionally charged. It is a work of the Italian sculptor Ciatone, and is made up of a large marble base in the shape of a cube.

On the front, within a hollow recess, Rudolf's head is represented in relief. Below this, carved in Latin characters, are his name, title and dates of birth and death. An angel lies on the cubic base, representing the soul of the dead. Behind him there is a broken Ionic column. The peacefulness of and of the forest and the serenity of the natural environment alleviated the Empress's pain each time she came here.

The Temple of Heine with, opposite, an old photograph of the Cenotaph of Rudolf.

D. THE LIFE OF ELISABETH

1

1. *Elisabeth on her coronation as Queen of Hungary. Georg Raab, Vienna 1867.*
2. *Posenhofen, Sissi's family home in Bavaria.*
3. *The Imperial weddings. Vienna, 1854.*
4. *Mayerling.*

She was born in Munich in 1837. Her father was the Philhellene Duke Maximilian Josef of Bavaria, of the Wittelsbach dynasty, and he passed on to her his admiration for ancient Greek civilisation.

Her mother was the Archduchess Ludovica. The young bright and sensitive Sissi, as Elisabeth was fondly known, was raised in a liberal environment with democratic principles. She grew up in a happy family atmosphere, and her childhood years were full of love and care in the Bavarian countryside, along with her sister Nene. This gave her a calm and a sweetness that can be seen in the expression on her face in all her portraits.

Among the great merits of her character were: her strong character, her conscience, her adherence to principles, her simplicity. She had the wonderful gift of being able to approach people and share things with them. Her romanticism and sensitivity often made her feel pain and weakness. Through her persistence and focus, however, she would once again be able to pull herself together. She was loyal to human values and ideals, and for this reason often clashed with powerful circles within the empire.

Her life was a romantic fairytale, with a happy beginning and a sad end. As fate would have it, the sweet Sissi passed into history as the Sad Empress.

When in 1854 she fell in love and married Franz Josef of the Hapsburg dynasty, her first cousin and son of her mother's sister, she was only seventeen years' old. Their wedding took place in Vienna with much imperial splendour. They had four children: Sofia, Gizela, Rudolf and, much later, Maria Valera.

In that day, the Austrian Empire included Hungary, Bohemia, Croatia, Dalmatia and northern Italy. Franz Josef was a powerful and busy monarch. He had, however, a great weakness for his young wife who, with the liberal sensibility that characterised her, often positively influenced his decisions, making them more sensitive to the needs of the people. This is why she was loved by the people in a way few other queens have been loved.

This situation, however, was not at all liked by the Queen Mother, the Archduchess Sofia, who disagreed with the ideas and actions of the young Elisabeth, and who was outraged by her influence over the Emperor. During a trip that the royal couple made to Italy, the Empress managed to convince Franz Josef to offer a general amnesty to the revolutionary Italians. This action was the last straw for Sofia, prompting much outrage on the part of the Queen Mother and her circles. She now tried to use every means to place things under her control again. Elisabeth felt suffocated by the strict etiquette of the Hapsburg court and the pressure and intimations from her mother-in-law. Even the way in which she raised her children had become a field of battle and antagonism between the two women.

Elisabeth wanted to pass on to her children her liberal models and human ideals, whilst Sofia insisted on bringing them up with steel character so that they could one day become strict monarchs.

One particular tragic event was the final blow for Elisabeth, and it cost her her mental health. In 1857, Elisabeth asked that their children go along with them on a visit that the royal couple was

2

3

4

Elisabeth and Franz Joseph at young age.

to make to Hungary. On this visit, their three-year-old daughter Sofia, their first-born child, suddenly died. The Archduchess then demanded guardianship over the little Gizela and the heir to the throne Rudolf. The Empress could not cope anymore, her jolted health worsened, and the doctors told her that she should distance herself from the heavy atmosphere of the palace in Vienna. She therefore decided to take a long journey in the Mediterranean, with the final destination of Madeira. She started out, then, from Ambersa in the royal yacht Victoria and Albert, which the Queen of England had given to her, for the beautiful Spanish island. She stayed there for five months in order to regain her psychological balance and relief from the pain of having lost her young daughter and being separated from her children. She managed to relax and make a good recovery and so decided to return to the palace. On the return journey, made in May 1861, she stopped off at Corfu and was captured by the heavenly nature of the island and the nobility of its residents. The island's beauty and its charming atmosphere had a positive affect on her psychology and convinced her that this was the most ideal place for her.

She returned to Corfu with her father at the end of June, and they remained here for quite a while as the guests of the British High Commissioner Sir Henry Storrs at his villa Mon Repo near Kanoni. She went for long walks in the garden, avoiding any formalities, and let her mind create the palace that she wanted to acquire here. Her beloved sister Nene came to see her to make her return to Austria. Franz Joseph followed in October of 1861, staying for only two days. He too was charmed by the place, and convinced that Elisabeth was in the most suitable place for her recovery.

After a while, Elisabeth went to Venice, where they brought her her children to

see. Being deprived of them had cost her dearly, so she decided to return to Vienna, tired from the journeys but in a good state of mind. A happy event, the birth of Maria Valeria, her last child, revitalised her. She was personally involved in the raising of Maria Valeria and this made her happy, whilst she also returned to her social and charitable activities, and even more energetically than before. She followed the political developments in the immense Empire, often intervening in the Emperor's work. Her sympathy for the Hungarian patriots who were struggling for their independence was quite clear, and was condemned by many circles. The Empress, however, was not daunted.

The defeat of Austria in the war with Prussia was followed by a rebellion on the part of the Hungarian autonomists. Elisabeth successfully exhorted her husband to give autonomy to the Hungarian people. Hungary was declared a Kingdom and the Austro-Hungarian Empire was established. On 8 June 1869, Franz Josef and Elisabeth were crowned King and Queen of Hungary. The Hungarian people adored their Queen, to whom they partly owed their independence. After the death of the Archduchess Sofia, Elisabeth engaged many Hungarian nobles in her service, something which particularly annoyed the Austrian aristocracy. The criticisms and rivalry from many of the circles within the Hapsburg court, in addition to the fateful blows that rocked her family from time to time made her seek relief once more through travel. Her family misfortunes came one after the other: her husband's brother, Maximillian the Emperor of Mexico, was executed by Mexican revolutionaries in 1867. His wife was committed to a psychiatric clinic. Her beloved cousin Ludovic II of Bavaria was found drowned in a lake. The young Mathilda, daughter of the Archduke Albert, was burnt to death.

Elisabeth left Vienna and started a never-ending journey, her own Odyssey. She went to England, France, Holland, Italy, Ireland, Greece, Turkey, Algeria, and the Middle East. In 1876 she started out with the royal yacht the Miramar for a visit to Athens and Corfu, to revive her love for Greece. During this difficult period of her life, she and Valeria would read the epics of Homer with a great passion, helped by the Greek teachers of the court. Of the contemporary writers, she loved Heine, Goethe, Schiller, Shakespeare and Byron. She too made her first timid effort at poetry with some lines that are on exhibit in the room with her mementoes in the Achillion.

She was amazed by Schliemann's excavations and made it her goal to visit the places where the Iliad and the Odyssey take place. She went to Corfu again in 1885, and was given a tour by the distinguished Greek scholar Baron Warsberg, the Austrian Consul on the island. She then visited Lefkada, Ithaka, Corinth, Zakynthos, Gytheio, Santorini and Athens, which she went to in order to rest for a while and to visit the Acropolis. She went on to Constantinople and Smyrna, although the military situation here prevented her from disembarking. She ended up at Troy, where she was completely entranced by Schliemann's finds from the mound of Hisarlik.

Elisabeth then continued on to Rhodes, Cyprus, Jerusalem, Port Said and Alexandria. On the return journey, she again passed through Corfu. Two years' later, she visited Lefkada and Ithaka with Warsberg, in the footsteps of Odysseus. 1888 was a very important year for Elisabeth in terms of the villa of Corfu. She had

1. *An old photograph of the gardens of the Achillion, from the room with the mementoes of Wilhelm II.*
2. *Prince Rudolf.*
3. *Elisabeth and Nene in Corfu.*

first visited the archaeological sites of Olympia and Mycenae, then passing through Nafplion and from there going to Corfu. Here she stayed with the widow of the Corfiot poet and diplomat Petros Vrailas Armenis in their villa near the village of Gastouri. The landscape enthused her greatly.

2

The next year, Elisabeth suffered the most serious trauma of her entire life. On 30 June 1889, her son Rudolf was found dead, along with his lover Maria Vetsera, in the hunting lodge of Mayerling, a little outside of Vienna. The heir to the throne, who was married to the Belgian princes Stefania, was having an affair with the beautiful Hungarian noblewoman. The reason for this double suicide, or assassination, are unknown, as the palace preferred to shroud the issue with a cloak of mystery in order not to undermine its status. It is said that Rudolf left a letter for his mother, revealing the reasons for his suicide, but the contents of that letter have been hushed up. Others say that they were murdered by circles opposed to Rudolf's liberal ideas, which his mother had implanted in him. Unfortunately, Elisabeth did not just lose a son - something unbearable for any mother - but she lost the person who was to continue her vision, as she herself believed. Rumours began to run rife within the court about the tragic deaths of the two young people. There then came the death of her sister, just to make things even worse for Elisabeth. Within this heavy climate, Valeria married, but this wedding was not enough to make things better for the sorrowful Empress.

3

Only her preoccupation with the building, furnishing and decoration of the Achillion - the land was purchased in the same year as Rudolf's death - made her forget things a little. She learnt Greek, and along with her teacher -distinguished intellectuals, such as Rousopoulos, Thermoyianni, Kefalas, Pallis and Papadopoulos- she would read and analyse the works of Homer and the great philosophers of antiquity.

In 1889, she engaged Constantine Christomanos, a philology graduate from the University of Vienna and author of the novel 'Kerenia Koukla' (Wax Doll), as her reader and teacher. He taught her the ancient and modern history of Greece and accompanied her on her travels. It is even said that a tender romance developed between them. In the 'Book of the Empress Elisabeth,' a diary of recollections that Christomanos published after her murder and which is exhibited along with other mementoes in the museum, the author gives a portrayal of her life and character. For nine years, she bore the sorrow from her son's death with her between Corfu and Vienna and, as she revealed to her daughter, she wished that she had died along with Rudolf.

1
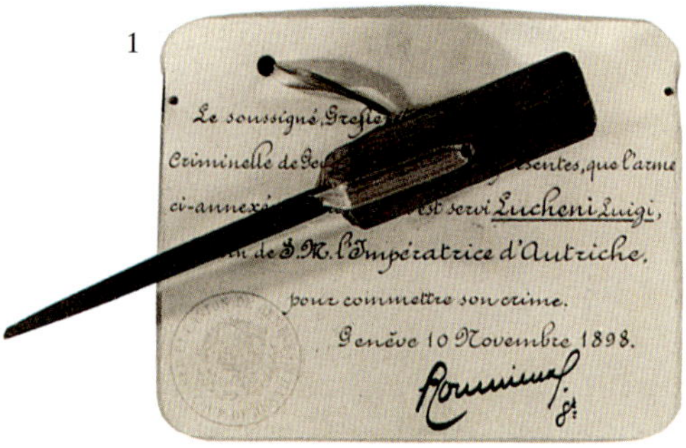

On 10 September 1898, the book of the Empress's much-afflicted life was finally closed with her own tragic death. She was in Geneva, outside the Beau Rivage hotel, with the escort of one of her ladies-in-waiting, yet without, as was her custom, a personal guard. An Italian anarchist worker, Luigi Lucheni, approached and stabbed her in the heart with a dagger. She died immediately. Her body was transported from Geneva to Vienna with a great honorary procession and with the escort of many ordinary people who loved the Empress and were grieving over her loss. Her funeral was carried out with the full honours fitting for a sensitive grandeur such as hers. The much-discussed Elisabeth finally found her peace in death. She was buried in the Capuchin monastery in Vienna, the burial place of the imperial family. The murderer committed suicide whilst in prison in 1910. Documents, photographs, photocopies, and sketches associated with her death and funeral can be seen in the room with her mementoes in the museum of the Achillion.

1. The lethal weapon with which Elisabeth was killed.
2. Elisabeth during her last visit to Corfu.

2

The villa on Corfu was inherited by Maria Valeria, remaining essentially uninhabited for ten whole years, until its purchase by Kaiser Wilhelm II. In this intervening period, Franz Josef had assigned responsibility for care and maintenance of the villa to Ferdinando Botempo, a former officer of the imperial yacht.

Elisabeth's stormy life has inspired many film scenarios. In 1956, the director Ernst Marischka made three films about her life - 'Sissi,' 'The Young Sissi' and 'Sissi the Empress' - starring Romy Schneider in the role of Elisabeth. In 1958, the same director also made the film 'Sissi' as a sequel to the two previous ones, with the same lead actress. In Luchino Visconti's film Ludwig, made in 1972, Romy Schneider for one more time plays Elisabeth. Rudolf's tragic death has also on occasion been presented on the big screen.

In the 1937 film 'Mayerling' by Anatole Litvak, with Danielle Darrieux and Charles Boyer. In 1948 with Jean Delannoy's 'Le Secret de Mayerling,' starring Jean Marais. And in 1978 with Terence Young's 'Mayerling,' starring Catherine Deneuve, Ava Gardner and Omar Sharif.

E. THE LIFE OF THE GERMAN EMPEROR WILHELM II AT THE ACHILLION

Wilhelm II on his yacht.

Kaiser Wilhelm II was born in 1859. He studied law and political sciences and underwent his military training at the Higher Military Academy of Germany. He was proclaimed Emperor of Germany and King of Prussia in 1888.

A physical handicap - his left arm was withered, which is why he is represented in paintings with his hand behind his back - did not prevent him from achieving in sports. He was an excellent equestrian and an experienced sailor. He travelled regularly on the imperial yacht the Hohenzollern and especially enjoyed steering himself.

When in 1889 his sister married the heir to the Greek throne Constantine, Wilhelm came to Athens for the wedding, continuing on to Corfu, where he was won over by the beauties of the place.

His next trip to the island took place several years later in 1905, as an official guest of the Greek royal family at the summer palace of Mon Repo. He made several excursions and visited the island's most impressive sights. Passing by the abandoned Achillion, he felt drawn by its history, captivated by the elegant building and the wild vegetation of the gardens, and sense a familiarity with the environment. He felt that the abandoned palace of the misfortunate Empress could be brought to life again and become a joyful summer palace for himself and his

1

family, and so decided to buy it. In 1907, then, after the standard procedures and legal formalities, he became the owner of the Achillion. He immediately charged that repairs, alterations and renovations be made. The House of the Knights was first built, on the designs of Ernst Ziller, in order to house his escort. The giant statue of the Victorious Achilles was set up on the site of the Dying Achilles, the statue of Heine was withdrawn and the sculpture of Elisabeth put in its place. The wall paintings in the stoa of the wise men were covered up with the plan of installing sculptures with mythological themes - a plan that was never realised. The furniture was added to and renewed with simpler pieces, ones fitting for a summer palace. A German botanist was engaged to look after the gardens. New plants were planted, beautiful flower beds created and flat gardens constructed. The sumptuous lighting within and outside the palace gave it an especial grandeur. The Bridge of the Kaiser was built at the port, which connected the pier with the gate to the entrance of the forest. By the spring of 1908 everything was ready to accept the new resident.

1. Old photograph with Wilhelm's yacht.

2. Franz Joseph receives Wilhelm II during the ceremony for the German Federal Rulers, to celebrate the 60 years of his reign. Sembun, Vienna (Franz von Matz).

The Kaiser with his wife Augusta Victoria, their daughter Victoria Louisa, and their sons Augustus Wilhelm and Oskar boarded the Hohenzollern at Venice, their destination their new villa in Corfu. The Greek royal family was there to welcome them.

The imperial family took great joy in the palace at Corfu. They always took great care to be there during Orthodox Easter as the Kaiser adored Greek customs and traditions. He stayed at the Achillion for a total of 162 days in six years and was very happy there. He would stroll around the garden on his own or with the gardener, he often took walks to places in the countryside, and went on excursions in his car - a strange site for the locals who had never before seen a car. He chatted with ordinary people and baptised the children of two Corfiots. One of the Emperor's most frequent trips was to Peleka. There is a plateau on the hill above the village that is shaped like a natural balcony. The Emperor often came here to admire the sunset, and this spot is known as the Emperor's Throne even today. The whole of the hinterland of the island as far as Corfu town, the olive groves in the north and the big blue of the Ionian Sea can be seen from this point.

Wilhelm received many important guests at the Achillion, including the prime ministers of Greece G. Theotokas and Eleftherios Venizelos.

The Emperor worshipped ancient Greek civilisation, but his great passion was archaeology. Corfu offered him many opportunities to pursue this interest. He gave his financial support to the archaeological excavations at the site of Ayii Theodori at Garitsa, where the gorgon from the pediment of the temple of Artemis was discovered. In order to assist the Greek government, which had taken on the enterprise, he invited the celebrated archaeologist Dörpfeld, Schliemann's assistant at Troy, over from Germany who, along with his Greek colleagues Professors Romaios and Versakis, proceeded to bring to light the ruins of the temple of Artemis. The collaboration between the three archaeologists continued at Kardaki, where the temple of Apollo was discovered. The excavations on the north-west beach of the island were terminated with the outbreak of the First World War in 1914. In one of the valuable photographs in the Achillion, we can see the Kaiser in among the archaeologists at the site, examining a find.

His interests were not limited to Ancient Greece, and he was equally fascinated by Greek folk culture and traditions. He loved traditional music and dance, admired the local costumes, enjoyed himself at the local festivals and organised parties in the palace gardens.

The First World War broke out in 1914. A year later Corfu was occupied by French and Serbian troops, and the Emperor's palace came into the hands of his enemies, who used it as a military headquarters and hospital, during which time it suffered much damage. Wilhelm, humiliated by his defeat, went into self-exile at Doorn in the Netherlands, and lived there in obscurity until his death in 1941.